Peace Warriors

Peace Warriors

RAYMOND HUBER

m

This book is copyright apart from any fair dealing as permitted under the Copyright Act, and no part may be reproduced without permission from the publisher.

Mākaro Press acknowledges all those who gave permission for the use of their words and images.

© Raymond Huber 2015
www.raymondhuber.co.nz

ISBN 978-0-9941172-2-9

A catalogue record for this book is available from the National Library of New Zealand

Cover design and illustration © Hugh Todd
www.constructedmeaning.com

Book design and typesetting: Paul Stewart
Editor: Mary McCallum

50% of royalties from the sale of this book donated to Oxfam NZ

m
Mākaro Press
PO Box 41-032 Eastbourne 5047
makaropress@gmail.com
makaropress.co.nz

Our books speak for themselves

Contents

FOREWORD	7
WHAT IS A PEACE WARRIOR?	9

War 11

The White Rose *Sophie Scholl*	13
The Non-Violent Village *Le Chambon*	19
IS WAR EVER RIGHT?	25
Arne and the War Machine *Arne Sejr*	27
CAN WAR BE PREVENTED?	31
Sold to Death *Archibald Baxter*	33
Hero to Zero *Ormond Burton*	41
WOULD I FIGHT TO SAVE MY FAMILY?	46
Asked to Kill *William White*	47

Weapons 51

Ships Against the Atom *Rainbow Warrior*	53
Tank Man *Tiananmen Square Protester*	61
ARE WE KILLER APES?	65
Blood and Bombers *Moana Cole*	67
CAN YOU BE PEACEFUL AND ANGRY?	72

Dictators — 73

Hitler's Birthday *Rosenstrasse Protesters* — 75

Facing the Generals *Aung San Suu Kyi* — 79

DOES PEOPLE POWER ALWAYS WORK? — 84

The Yellow Revolution
People power in the Philippines — 85

Protest — 89

Salt versus Bullets *Mahatma Gandhi* — 91

SHOULD PEACE PROTESTERS BREAK THE LAW? — 96

Little Rock Nine *Elizabeth Eckford* — 97

The Lions Rage *Te Whiti* — 103

The Disappeared *Mothers of Plaza de Mayo* — 107

TINA OR TARA? — 111

To Create not Destroy
Lois White, Rita Angus, Johnny Johnson — 115

Talking about Peacebuilding — 123

MORE DISCUSSION QUESTIONS — 125

GLOSSARY — 128

Foreword

Professor Kevin P Clements
Director, National Centre for Peace and Conflict Studies

WAR HEROES ARE HONOURED FOR ACTS OF BRAVERY IN the face of fire, but there are many others who boldly choose the path of non-violence. To stand up for one's beliefs is not a simple thing; it requires strength and courage. All the people in this book were able to resist strong social pressures to conform and obey those in power. They could do so because they had deep personal beliefs and values, the courage of their convictions and social support for their non-violent resistance. All believed in non-violence and the power of friendly persuasion, and the importance of affirming life and love in the face of destructive forces.

It's essential that there will always be individuals and groups who have a commitment to peace and non-violence. Without them, the violence and military structures of the world would be unchallenged. Those who oppose war and support peace are creating a space where non-military options can be discussed and used before force.

I commend this book to all who wish to live their lives non-violently and without weapons. It provides inspirational stories for your journey.

What is a Peace Warrior?

Watch the tv news and you'll see bombs exploding in crowded cities and soldiers shooting people. It seems that violence is an unstoppable force, so it might surprise you that there's also great power in peace. This book has stories of peace warriors who have changed the course of history:

- The small-town boy who stood up to Hitler.

- A high school student who faced a racist mob.

- Mothers who protest weekly against a brutal military dictatorship.

- A whole town that used non-violence to save thousands.

- The ship that sailed towards a nuclear test.

A peace warrior is a person who fights for peace and justice without using violence. A peace warrior can be a soldier who refuses to kill, a student who protests or a parent who stands up to a brutal government. Just as a war hero risks his or her life in battle, a peace warrior shows courage in the struggle for peace. A peace warrior is an active peace-builder.

When peace warriors join together in large groups it's known as people power. People power is seen in protest marches, worker strikes, mass disobedience of unjust laws, and even in elections. Sometimes a whole town or country can practise non-violent people power.

Is it true? *Peace Warriors* is based on recorded history, but that's not the whole story. We can be sure of facts such as dates and places, but people's thoughts and feelings are often not recorded by history – so I've imagined what it was like to be present at key events and have dramatised these in my own words. These sections are in italics. The book also focuses on pivotal moments in people's lives not their whole lives or whole events. To get a fuller picture, we have included a list of books, films and online resources at the end of each chapter that will help you find out more.

War

GERMANY

The White Rose

IMAGINE LIVING IN A COUNTRY WHERE YOU CAN BE arrested for listening to the wrong radio station, and it's against the law to make jokes about the government. This was Germany where Sophie Scholl grew up in the 1930s. She was 12 years old when Adolf Hitler and his Nazi Party began to rule. At first young people were excited about Hitler's new government, and most of them joined boys' and girls' groups called the Hitler Youth. Sophie enjoyed her group because they went on outdoor camps and did sports such as swimming and gymnastics. But the Nazi's rule of terror was on the rise.

Sophie Scholl.

Jewish books were banned, Jews were attacked on the streets and the Hitler Youth taught that Jews were bad. Sophie was shocked, but she stood by her Jewish friends and stubbornly read the banned books. The Nazis arrested anyone who protested against them – about five per cent of the German population was locked up in the 1930s for anti-government behaviour.

When the Second World War started Sophie went to study at Munich University. There she joined a secret group called the White Rose, along with her brother Hans. The group of six young people were inspired by black students in America who were using non-violent protests. The White Rose wanted to speak out against Nazi crimes such as the murder of Jews and disabled people. It organised discussion groups for other students and graffitied campus walls with the German word 'Freiheit', meaning 'Freedom'.

The group printed thousands of leaflets exposing the Nazis and encouraging people to resist them in their daily lives. They delivered the leaflets to houses at night, and posted them to addresses chosen at random, so nothing could be traced back to the group. Sophie was in charge of buying paper and stamps and Hans wrote most of the leaflets. Here are some extracts from the White Rose leaflets:

> Every word that proceeds from Hitler's mouth is a lie. When he says peace, he means war.
>
> Our present State is a dictatorship of Evil. 'We've known that for a long time,' I can hear you say,

> 'and it is not necessary for you to remind us of it once again.' So I ask you: If you are aware of this, why do you not stir yourselves?
>
> Because every day that you delay, every day that you do not resist this spawn of hell, your guilt is steadily increasing.
>
> Do not forget that every nation deserves the government that it endures.
>
> Many, perhaps most of the readers of these leaflets are not certain how they can practise resistance ... We will attempt to show you that every person is in a position to contribute something to the overthrow of this system.

It was a dangerous thing to write these words because anyone who stood up to the Nazis could be put in prison or executed. The White Rose message spread around Germany and the secret police, the Gestapo, were desperate to find them. But they had no idea where to look or even how big the White Rose organisation was ...

It is 1943 ...

It's early morning and Sophie and Hans have finished breakfast. On the floor are piles of White Rose leaflets, almost 2,000 Hans reckons. They sit down and load the forbidden leaflets into a large suitcase. Hans carries the suitcase as they walk to Munich University in the cool winter air. The plan is to leave the leaflets in the corridors while the students are still in the classrooms. Sophie and

Hans know the building well, so it should be quick and easy.

They enter the university and hurry up the huge marble staircase from floor to floor, placing piles of leaflets as they go. On each floor Sophie and Hans race along the corridors and drop leaflets outside the classrooms. They reach the third floor and Sophie looks up at the clock at the top of the big staircase. She suddenly realises they're running late and the students will pour out in a minute. They return to the top of the stairs, but there's one small pile of leaflets left over. Sophie flicks the leaflets out into the air and they dance like butterflies, down, down to the courtyard below.

At that moment the students come from their rooms and look up in wonder at the rain of paper. But a caretaker is also standing in the courtyard and grabs a leaflet. The words 'Hitler's mouth is a lie' jump out at him.

He sees two students at the top of the stairs and shouts, 'Stop! Stop!' He runs up the stairs towards them.

Sophie and Hans are trapped. They know the caretaker is a diehard Nazi and he will certainly call the Gestapo. But they don't run away.

The members of the White Rose were arrested. Sophie and Hans were immediately tried by the Nazi judge, Roland Freisler, who was famous for screaming at people in his courtroom. Sophie and Hans were found guilty, and were beheaded by guillotine just four days after their arrest.

Hans was 25 and Sophie was 21 years old.

Sophie Scholl and her friends stood up to one of the most violent states in history. Today in Germany there are many schools and streets named after Sophie, and she's called one of the greatest German women of all time. At Munich University the courtyard is now covered in tiles with images of the last leaflets that she threw into the air.

Events

1921	Sophie Scholl born
1933	Nazi rule begins
1938	Night of the Broken Glass: Jews attacked in public places
1939	Second World War begins
1942–43	White Rose leaflets printed
1943	Six members of the White Rose executed
1945	Second World War ends: 55 million killed, mostly civilians, including 6 million Jews murdered

Find out more

Online: Holocaust Education & Archive Research Team
www.holocaustresearchproject.org/revolt/scholl.html

Online: Leaflets of the White Rose translated by Ruth Sachs, www.white-rose-studies.org /The_Leaflets.html

Read: *Sophie Scholl, The Real Story of the Woman who Defied Hitler* by Frank McDonough, The History Press, 2010.

Watch: *Sophie Scholl – The Final Days* (GERMANY, 2005).

....
Sophie Scholl photo credit: Holocaust Education & Archive Research Team. White Rose leaflets quote credit: Leaflets of the White Rose, translated by Ruth Sachs.

The Non-Violent Village

THIS IS THE STORY OF PEOPLE POWER IN WARTIME. A mountain village in southern France saved thousands of Jews from certain death during the Second World War. The Jews were refugees, escaping from the Nazis who were murdering them all over Europe. At the time there were few countries that offered to protect the Jews, and some actively helped the Nazis capture them.

Germany invaded France at the start of the war, and the French government helped them by arresting Jews and sending them to death camps. However, the entire village of Le Chambon chose to hide Jews and other refugees – giving them false identities and disguising them as locals. It was dangerous because it was against the law to help Jews and to make fake documents.

The French government put 40,000 Jews into holding camps, ready to be deported to Germany.

Peace Warriors

Jewish children sheltered in the town of Le Chambon, 1941.

The village of Le Chambon was well placed to rescue them: it was on an isolated plateau, with a network of children's homes and a pacifist school at its heart. The school was started by Pastor André Trocmé, a church leader who taught non-violent resistance to the students and encouraged the villagers to welcome refugees. The first acts of resistance were by school students who refused to salute the new government's flag or to sign an oath of loyalty.

The village leaders arranged for many Jews, most of them children, to be secretly released from camps and brought to the village. The villagers welcomed the refugees into their homes and gave them clothes and work.

News of the village spread and refugees came from far and wide, but it wasn't long before the French police staged a raid ...

The Non-Violent Village

It is 1942 ...

Fifty armed policemen roar into the town square on motorbikes and in trucks. They line up beside their vehicles making sure to display machine guns. The villagers slowly gather around and the police captain demands that they hand over their Jews. No one moves for a minute, and the captain warns that anybody caught hiding Jews will be sent to prison.

Then Pastor Trocmé steps forward and speaks: 'We don't know if there are any Jews living here, and if we did know we wouldn't tell you.'

The angry captain orders his men to search the town from top to bottom. The police go from house to house, examining ID cards, scouring attics and basements, and looking for secret compartments. They find nothing. What the police don't know is that at the first sign of the raid the locals hid the Jews. Some are in nearby forests, others on remote farms.

The police don't give up, and for the next three weeks they search the town and the surrounding area.

The villagers stay one step ahead, moving Jews from place to place to avoid searchers. Finally the police arrest a man who they say is a Jew (although only his grandparents are Jewish). The man is put into a truck and the villagers crowd around. A boy walks up to the police and asks to give the prisoner some food. He's allowed to give the man a piece of rare wartime chocolate. Food is severely restricted, especially luxury items.

Now more people come forward and give gifts of food. The police convoy leaves and the town can breathe again.

There were many other raids on Le Chambon during the war but few Jews were captured. Sometimes the villagers would get advance warning of a raid, and the local Boy Scout group would be sent out to spread the word to hide the Jews. Some children didn't need to hide at all and simply blended in with their playmates on the street.

What was the secret of Le Chambon's success? Very few people were told where all the Jews were living, and nobody in the village would betray a refugee. This was a strongly Christian district and they believed that it was wrong to turn away a person in need. It also helped that the village was on an isolated plateau – and the surrounding farms and villages helped hide refugees. Le Chambon eventually got support from the wider world as aid groups and governments sent money and supplies.

By 1943 there were more Germans in the area, including the dreaded Gestapo, the secret police. There were more raids on Le Chambon, some village leaders were arrested, and the local doctor was executed. One day the Gestapo raided a school and took away five Jewish children and their teacher – they were all murdered in a death camp. German troops took over the main hotel in the village for the rest of the war, but remained unaware that they were surrounded by Jewish refugees. It became harder and harder to hide people and the villagers arranged for many Jews to escape to Switzerland.

Altogether, Le Chambon and the surrounding district sheltered about 3,000 refugees. A similar act of people power happened in the Dutch village of Nieuwlande in 1943 – every one of the 117 households hid Jewish families from the Nazis.

> 'Le Chambon became the safest place for Jews in Europe.'
> Philip P Hallie

Events

1939	Second World War begins
1940–44	Germany occupies France
1940	Internment camps in France begin to be used to hold Jews for transportation to Nazi death camps
1945	Second World War ends

Find out more

Read: *Village of Secrets: Defying the Nazis in Vichy France* by Caroline Moorehead, Chatto & Windus, 2014.

Read: *Lest Innocent Blood Be Shed* by Philip P Hallie, Harper Collins, 1994.

Online: US Holocaust Memorial Museum (Holocaust Encyclopedia) www.ushmm.org

Peace Warriors

....
Jewish children in Le Chambon photo credit: US Holocaust Memorial Museum. Phillip P Hallie quote credit: *Lest Innocent Blood Be Shed.*

Is war ever right?

It is wrong to kill a human being, and yet soldiers kill people in wartime. Why? Because the rules of right and wrong become unclear in a war. Soldiers believe they must kill to defeat their enemy. This is why many people fought in the Second World War: Hitler's army had invaded several countries and, in the end, war was the only way to stop him. It was called a 'just war' because it was in self-defence. It succeeded, but at a huge cost, including mass bombings of English, German and Japanese cities.

Some 'rules' have been suggested for a just war:
1. It must be for a just cause, for example, to prevent genocide.
2. A decision to go to war must be based on accurate information.
3. It should be a last resort after all non-violent solutions have been tried.
4. Every effort must be made to avoid harming civilians.

Few wars have been truly just. Most are fought for the wrong reasons and they're never limited to soldiers fighting soldiers. The innocent suffer as well.

Over 60 million civilians were killed in the wars of the 20th century compared to about 40 million military personnel who died. War also creates millions of homeless and damages the environment.

'The war against Nazism was a justified war, although not everything done in it by the opponents of Nazism was justified.'

AC Grayling

Find out more

Online: 198 Methods of Non-Violent Action
www.aforcemorepowerful.org

AC Grayling quote credit: *The Reason of Things: Living with Philosophy* by AC Grayling, Phoenix, 2010.

DENMARK

Arne and the War Machine

How did a small-town boy fight the biggest war machine in history armed only with his wits? The Second World War was the most destructive of all time, but the people of Denmark proved that non-violence can resist a powerful army. The Germans, led by Adolf Hitler, invaded many countries across Europe. When they took over Denmark, the German army ordered the Danish people to work for them. They wanted to use Denmark's factories and farms to supply the German army with weaponry and food.

Arne Sejr was a student in the town of Slagelse when the invaders arrived in force …

It is 1940 …

Eighteen-year-old Arne Sejr is angry. There are Germans swarming all over his town. He can't walk down the streets of Slagelse without seeing soldiers waving their guns about, and Arne hates the way they bark orders at unarmed people. Germans have taken over the shops and factories, and every classroom has a photo of the hated Hitler on the wall.

Arne felt helpless when the German army invaded Denmark and he wondered how he could possibly fight back, but now his anger gives him an idea. It's simple but dangerous: don't cooperate with the Germans.

Arne gets out a typewriter and makes a list of ideas for resisting the Germans. He thinks of ways people can protest in their daily lives such as:

> *Work slowly for the German occupiers*
> *Slow down all means of transport*
> *Don't attend German films or read their newspapers*
> *Don't buy things at German shops*

Arne types the list as fast as he can and ends up with 25 copies. He sets off in the early morning and secretly delivers his list to the mailboxes of the town's leaders.

The war drags on for years, and Arne's list of ideas is copied and passed from hand to hand around the whole of Denmark, inspiring unarmed people to resist the German invaders.

Arne's protest did not stop there. He also organised a resistance group for high school and university students. Arne was arrested and tortured by Hitler's secret police but he escaped and continued his struggle to free Denmark.

The Danish government also found clever ways to sabotage the Germans. In 1943 they organised nationwide strikes where workers put down their tools. The Germans then took over the government but the strikes continued, including a whole month when the entire country stopped work. The army threatened the striking workers with tanks and guns, and they cut off water and power supplies. But the strikers held on and the army backed off. The workers succeeded in slowing down the supply of war materials to Germany.

People resisted the invaders in many creative ways: students in schools refused to speak German, communities held 'Songfests' to celebrate Danish music and culture, and others marched in the streets. To spread the word about protest events, millions of copies of a secret newspaper were printed and handed out around the country.

The biggest threat to life came in 1943 when the Germans ordered the arrest of all the Jews in Denmark. Hitler had set up death camps for the mass murder of Jews throughout Europe. If Jews were arrested it meant almost certain death for them. When news of the order got out, ordinary people all over Denmark sheltered Jews in homes, hospitals, and churches. They were smuggled to safety in Sweden in every kind of boat including trawlers, ferries, rowboats and kayaks. Arne's student resistance group also helped with smuggling people out of Denmark. Almost all of the 8,000 Danish Jews were saved.

'The Danes challenged the most barbaric regime of the modern period and did so not with troops or tanks but with singing, striking, going home to garden, and standing in public squares.'
Peter Ackerman & Jack DuVall

Events

1933	Hitler's rule begins in Germany
1939	Second World War begins when Germany invades Poland
1940	Germany invades Denmark
1943	Jews smuggled out of Denmark
1945	Second World War ends

Find out more

Read: *A Force More Powerful: A Century of Nonviolent Conflict* by Peter Ackerman and Jack DuVall, Palgrave MacMillan, 2001.

Online: Denmark, Living With The Enemy www.aforcemorepowerful.org/films/afmp/stories/denmark.php

....

Peter Ackerman & Jack DuVall quote credit: *A Force More Powerful: A Century of Nonviolent Conflict.*

Can war be prevented?

Some countries go to war before they have tried the many non-violent alternatives. Here are some actions which could be used before bullets and bombs:

- negotiate and persuade
- block international trade in weapons
- block investment in war-related industry
- organise mass protests
- send in United Nations Peacekeepers

Most wars happen in poor countries. Money spent on war would be better spent fighting poverty. The world's military spending is currently US$1,747 billion a year, and it has increased over the past 20 years. A tiny fraction of that, about US$30 billion, could feed the hungry people of the world for a year; and a little more would provide health care and education for those in need.

Peace warriors are people that constantly remind governments of the alternatives to war.

Find out more

Online: Oxfam Peacebuilding and Conflict Prevention. www.oxfam.org.nz

Online: Spending On War www.sipri.org

FRANCE

Sold to Death

WHAT HAPPENS WHEN A SOLDIER REFUSES TO FIGHT? It sometimes happens in wartime, in the heat of battle, or when people are forced to join the military. In the First World War, men who refused to fight were officially known as conscientious objectors, but people often called them 'cowards' and 'parasites'.

Conscientious objectors believed shooting people in a war was the same as murder. Thousands of them were put in prison for refusing to take part in the war. The First World War was a terrible waste of life. One after the other, countries were drawn into it because they had signed agreements to help each other. Soldiers fought a series of bloody battles in the fields of France, fighting from trenches that they dug specially.

Here's the story of one young man from Otago, New Zealand, who refused to join the army. Archie Baxter was 17 when he decided that the war was wrong because killing was wrong. New Zealand soldiers had gone to fight in a war in South Africa, but Archie became a pacifist after hearing a lawyer speaking out against that war. He was so confident that he talked his family of ten into following his anti-war stand.

At the outbreak of the First World War, thousands of New Zealanders crowded the streets to celebrate. People wanted to fight with 'Mother England' because they had relatives there. Many young men volunteered to fight, but as the war dragged on they became less enthusiastic. The government introduced a law called conscription that said men aged over 18 had to join the army. Archie and five of his brothers refused to join up and were arrested. Soldiers marched Archie and other objectors through the streets of Dunedin to shame them. He hated being treated like a criminal in his home town.

Archie was sent to prison several times, until finally he and a few other objectors were shipped to Europe. At first he was imprisoned in England where they tried to talk him into fighting. Here is Archie writing in his book *We Will Not Cease*. He is describing how a prison doctor talked to him:

> 'You're far too good a Highlander, Baxter,' he said, 'not to be fighting for your king. When you get to France you'll be throwing Germans over your head on your bayonet.'
>
> 'Yes, my ancestors fought for the king … I'm fighting too, only … I'm fighting against a war.'

> 'Oh well,' he said, 'they might get you a job rocking cradles.'
>
> 'If people of your views run the world,' I answered, 'there soon won't be any cradles to rock.'

Archie stubbornly refused to change his mind. The army was worried by this man, because they knew that if Baxter's anti-war belief spread then other soldiers might also refuse to fight. Without soldiers there would be no war. To try and break his spirit, they sent Archie to the battlefront in France in 1918 where the war had ground on for almost four years. Here's how he described the battlefield in his book:

> The cemetery of a million men! ... the yawning mouths of the countless shell holes were ready to suck in the living men who moved day and night among them like maggots in the slime.

The officers at the front tried to force Archie into co-operating with the army. He was tied to a post outside for several hours a day, the ropes so tight his hands turned black.

How did he survive such torture? Partly because of his inner strength and partly because Archie felt supported by the fellow soldiers who admired his courage. However, some of the officers beat Archie and one day a brutal sergeant dragged him out onto the battlefield to get rid of him for good …

New Zealand trench, Gommecourt, France, 1918.

It is 1918 ...

Archie stands in a muddy trench. The sergeant grabs him by the arm.

'Get up, Baxter,' he snaps. 'There's only one cure for a man who can't be broken.' He pulls Archie up a rickety ladder, over the top of the trench, and onto the battlefield. 'I hope a shell gets you and blows you to your maker!' the red-faced sergeant yells, and sprints back to the trenches.

Archie is left standing in the battlefield. The ground is pocked with smoking craters as far as the eye can see. Barbed wire sprouts like skeletal bushes. He kicks at a branch sticking out of the ground and shudders when he recognises it as the blackened leg of a horse.

A distant thud, a screech overhead and a shell bursts. Earth explodes – a shock wave punches Archie's eardrums – he spits dirt. Archie wipes his brow and sees blood smeared across the back of his hand. A metal splinter from the shell has grazed his head. Of course he hasn't been given a helmet because the sergeant expects him to die out here.

In the silence before the next explosion Archie recalls a striking dream he'd had years before the war: a dream of a forest of tall trees. He knew that the trees were all the young men in the world, and the forest had been sold to Death.

Archie realises he's standing beside an ammunition dump. If a shell hits it, he will indeed be blown to the heavens.

The calm is broken by the screams of shells heading in his direction. A storm of explosions bursts around Archie and mud and sticks rain down. When the smoke clears a little, Archie is stunned to find that he is still alive.

Archibald Baxter.

After that, Archie spent more and more time in the trenches. Then, after a forced march, he collapsed in exhaustion and was returned to New Zealand. He married Millicent Brown and they were active in anti-war protests for their whole lives. Their son James K Baxter became a famous poet.

'If there were no conscientious objectors, nobody saying no to war anywhere, there would be no restraints on those who would choose military solutions to problems.'
Kevin Clements

Events

1882	Archibald Baxter born
1899–1902	Boer War, South Africa: 75,000 killed
1914–18	First World War: 15 million killed
1970	Archibald Baxter dies

Find out more

Read: *We Will Not Cease* by Archibald Baxter, Cape Catley, 1980.

Watch: *Field Punishment No.1* (TVNZ, 2014).

Online: Archibald Baxter Memorial Trust
www.archibaldbaxtertrust.com

....

Kevin Clements quote: kevinclementspeaceandconflict.wordpress.com. Archibald Baxter quote credit: *We Will Not Cease* by Archibald Baxter, Cape Catley, 1980. Trenches photo credit: Alexander Turnbull Library, Wellington, NZ. Ref: ½-013485-G. Archibald Baxter photo credit: Archibald Baxter Memorial Trust.

NEW ZEALAND

Hero to Zero

It is 1942 …

The heavy prison door clangs shut behind Ormond, the final clunk of the lock like a stab in his back. The concrete walls seem to close in on him. This chilly cell is to be home for the next two and a half years – his living room, bedroom, office and toilet. Ormond measures out two short paces between the walls. He sits on the thin mattress and touches the crusty pillow, baked hard to kill off lice.

The first thing he does is write to his wife, Helen. Being separated from her will be the worst thing about being locked up. Prison won't be easy, but Ormond's life hasn't been either. He'll never forget the horror of the First World War – dragging the bloodied bodies of his mates from the mud, patching their wounds as best he could. He had returned home from that war as a Kiwi hero. People cheered, wanted to shake the hand of a brave man, and the government pinned medals on his chest.

Peace Warriors

Now the unbelievable has happened: another world war is destroying millions of lives. This time Ormond sits in prison, the cheers replaced by the clank of doors along the cell block. He's gone from hero to zero. Why has his country rejected him?

A war hero can be a soldier who shows bravery by fighting, but it can also be one who actively resists violence: Ormond Burton was both. Ormond was a First World War hero but New Zealanders turned against him. To understand why, you need to know how he was changed by war. As a young man he trained as a teacher and when the war came, 21-year-old Ormond was sent straight to Gallipoli, in Turkey. He first served with the Field Ambulance, a group of soldiers who cared for the wounded and dying, then in France as a soldier.

Ormond was a courageous fighter who was wounded several times and had some miraculous escapes from death. He came home to New Zealand in 1919 wearing two medals for bravery under fire, one awarded by the French government. But Ormond had seen the slaughter of so many young lives; most terribly in the battle of the Somme where 100,000 men were killed or wounded.

Ormond wrote: 'War is just waste and destruction, solving no problems but creating new and terrible ones.' The tough soldier became a fierce pacifist, and told other young men that they should reject the

Ormond Burton (left) on the front line of the Somme, France, 1918.

army. His non-violence spilled over into the teaching job in the 1920s. In those days, all males over the age of eleven had to do army training at school – and Ormond persuaded his school to stop army-style training. He also talked many teachers out of hitting children with a cane as a punishment. Ormond was ahead of his time – compulsory military training was abolished in 1958, with selective service until 1972. School caning wasn't banned until 1990.

Ormond became a church leader, and he and his wife, Helen, set up a house for the homeless in Wellington in the 1930s. He helped to form the Christian Pacifist Society, and as the Second World War loomed the group took their peaceful protest into public places. Ormond made speeches, marched in the streets, and wrote anti-war pamphlets. But there was very little support for anti-war protesters and the church expelled him. Most Kiwis thought it was right go to war again. When war was declared Ormond protested outside government buildings in Wellington.

Speaking against the war was against the law and Ormond was swiftly arrested. When asked by a police officer if he had any identifying marks, Ormond, the war hero, replied: 'Gunshot wound left chest, bayonet wound left knee, shrapnel wounds right leg, gunshot wound left arm.'

He was put in prison. The government were worried that Ormond, as a well-known soldier, might persuade other men not to fight. The deputy prime minister went to see Ormond in prison and asked him to stop speaking out, but Ormond refused. Again and again he spoke in public and each time he was fined or imprisoned: including eleven months hard labour and, finally, two and a half years in prison.

The government introduced conscription again and most men were forced to join the army. Eight hundred pacifists were locked in detention camps during the war.

In the 1960s Ormond protested against New Zealand fighting in the Vietnam War. His life spanned three horrific wars that New Zealand was involved in. He was not afraid to speak about peace when it was not popular to do so.

Events

1893	Ormond Burton born
1914–18	First World War: 15 million killed
1939–45	Second World War: 55 million killed
1958	Compulsory military training abolished in New Zealand
1960–75	Vietnam War: 3.5 million killed
1961–72	Selective military training in New Zealand for 20 year olds
1974	Ormond Burton dies

Find out more

Read: *I Can Do No Other: A Biography of the Reverend Ormond Burton* by Ernest A Crane, Hodder & Stoughton, 1986.

Read: 'War and the peacemaker' by Andrew Stone, *NZ Herald*, 19 April 2014. Available at www.nzherald.co.nz

Listen online: Recording of Ormond Burton www.teara.govt.nz/en/speech/119/burton-talking-about-christmas-in-1943

....

Ormond Burton quote credit: *I Can Do No Other: A Biography of the Reverend Ormond Burton* by Ernest A Crane. Ormond Burton on the front line in the Somme photo credit: Alexander Turnbull Library, Wellington, NZ. Ref: ½-013092-G.

Would I fight to save my family?

There's a little story sometimes used to support the idea of war. Imagine a burglar breaks into my house and threatens my family – surely I would fight to save them. In the same way, it's argued that if a country is attacked, surely it should fight back.

The plot of any story has many possible endings. Yes, I'd do absolutely everything in my power to protect my family. I might try and restrain or disarm the intruder. I could negotiate with him or I could help my family escape or hide. But I'd definitely call the police.

What I would not do is kill the burglar, go to his home and kill his family, burn down his house and then bomb his entire neighbourhood. In the same way, wars always kill the innocent; they're never limited to soldiers fighting each other.

It's up to us to choose how the story ends.

AUSTRALIA

Asked to Kill

THE VIETNAM WAR WAS ONE OF THE MOST CRUEL IN recent times. It began as a civil war between North and South Vietnam, but then the United States sided with the South and joined in the fighting during the 1960s. Innocent people were targeted and a fire-bomb called napalm was used on them. Three-and-a-half million people were killed in the war, most of them Vietnamese civilians. The US also sprayed a toxic chemical called Agent Orange over the country to kill the vegetation, removing both shelter and food crops.

Countries that were friends with the US joined in the war, including Australia and New Zealand. One reason Australia joined in was a fear of being invaded by Asian countries. It sent 50,000 troops to Vietnam, and introduced a law requiring young men to join the army when they turned 20. The penalty for breaking the law was prison. Not all men had to join at once

Peace Warriors

Anti-Vietnam War protesters, 1967.

– they were chosen by a Lotto-style draw called the 'birthday ballot'. Marbles representing birth dates were taken from a barrel, and those selected went to Vietnam – an unhappy birthday gift.

In 1966, a young teacher named William White became the focal point of Australian protests against the war. During the year William turned 20 and was selected by the birthday ballot to go to Vietnam. He refused and was fired from the school where he worked.

William strongly believed that war was wrong.

The army threatened him with 'severe punishments' if he didn't report for military duty, and he got the attention of the news media because he was a respected teacher who couldn't be labelled as another hippy protester. One day, the police came to William's house, dragged him outside and arrested him in front of a crowd of reporters. The army then offered William a way out: if he agreed to join them, he'd be given non-fighting duties.

William refused because he didn't want even the smallest part in helping drive the war machine. He took his case to court but the judge rejected it, saying William's anti-war ideas were 'the result of ignorance'. He was sentenced to 21 days in prison.

William became an inspiration for the peace movement and there was an increase in anti-Vietnam War protests, both in Australia and New Zealand. The largest protests were in 1970 when tens of thousands of people across the world joined in marches. Troops began to withdraw from Vietnam soon after. Australia's death toll from the war was 500, New Zealand's was 39 – and in later years many soldiers got sick or died because of exposure to Agent Orange.

Events

1946	William White born
1954	War between North and South Vietnam begins
1965–68	Operation Rolling Thunder: continuous bombing of Vietnam
1965	200,000 US troops invade Vietnam
1966	William White selected to go to Vietnam
1969	500,000 US troops now in Vietnam
1969–70	Large anti-war demonstrations
1973	US troops withdraw from Vietnam

Find out more

Read: *Red Haze: Australia and New Zealand in Vietnam* by Leon Davidson, Black Dog Books, 2006.

Online: American experience in the Vietnam War
www.pbs.org/wgbh/amex/vietnam/

Online: NZ experience in the Vietnam War
www.nzhistory.net.nz/war/vietnam-war

....
Vietnam War protest photo credit: Lyndon B Johnson Library.

Weapons

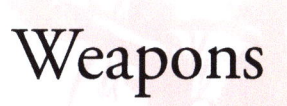

Ships Against the Atom

How could peaceful protest succeed against the deadliest weapons ever invented? The nuclear age began in 1945 when the United States dropped an atomic bomb on the city of Hiroshima, killing 70,000 people in a single second. Tens of thousands more Japanese civilians died later from radiation sickness. The blast began a race between countries to make their own nuclear weapons, until by the 1970s there were enough to destroy all life on Earth.

The United States, Britain and France tested their nuclear weapons on isolated islands in the Pacific Ocean, hoping they'd be ignored, but they weren't. A wave of anger about nuclear testing swept the planet and the anti-nuclear movement was born.

France exploded hundreds of nuclear bombs on Mururoa Atoll in the Pacific. Australia and New

Nuclear test at Bikini Atoll.

Zealand took legal action against France in the World Court, which ruled that the blasts had to stop, but the French government ignored the Court and kept testing its bombs. After that, many ordinary people took part in a new, daring protest: sailing small boats into the nuclear test zone.

The protests aimed to attract media attention and hopefully stop the tests as well – surely the French wouldn't blow up unarmed boats. Yachts from around the world sailed into the danger zone, and New Zealand even sent two navy ships to the test area. All this forced the French to move their tests underground on Mururoa.

The environmental group Greenpeace organised many anti-nuclear protests. Its ship, the *Rainbow*

Warrior, went on a protest voyage in 1985 around the Pacific with an international crew of 15. They sailed first to tiny Rongelap Atoll which had been poisoned by American nuclear tests at nearby Bikini Atoll. The crew were shocked to find the islanders were still suffering from radiation effects 30 years after the blasts (including cancers and birth defects). They were desperate to get off the toxic island, so the crew relocated the whole population to a cleaner island – 300 people in all – along with their dismantled houses, and their chickens and pigs.

Next the *Rainbow Warrior* went to Kwajalein Atoll where the Americans were developing 'Star Wars' weapons to place on satellites. The crew sneaked onto the base and put up a huge banner:

'We can't relocate the world … stop Star Wars.'

Then they sailed to Auckland to prepare for a trip to Mururoa …

It is 1985 …

Two men in wetsuits stand on the shore of Auckland harbour, almost invisible in the evening gloom. They make sure they are alone and drag a small inflatable boat into the water. The men sling in their backpacks and diving tanks. Together they lift a heavy black bag off the

Peace Warriors

sand and lower it into the boat, but their hands are wet and the bag slips and bumps against the boat's motor.

'Mon Dieu!' says one man, and they wait for their hands to stop shaking.

They are French Secret Service agents and their mission is to blow up an old trawler anchored nearby. The men clamber into their boat, the motor purrs and the spies set off into the night. Within minutes they near the target – the ship is tied up at a wharf. Lights illuminate the name on its side: Rainbow Warrior. *They cut the motor and drift closer.*

The men open the black bag and gingerly remove their 'babies' – two bombs packed with enough explosives to send the ship to the bottom. They put on masks and tanks and slide beneath the water. On board the ship, the crew are in the middle of a meeting. Nobody inside the cabin hears the soft clunk of the limpet bombs being attached beneath them.

One of the *Rainbow Warrior*'s engineers was 25-year-old Hanne Sorensen. Growing up in Denmark, Hanne had been interested in social issues, and when a Greenpeace ship visited her home port, she knew she had to take action. She joined Greenpeace in protests against whaling and the dumping of toxic waste.

Hanne describes what happened the night of the bombing:

> There was a whole peace flotilla being prepared for Mururoa Atoll. I had been working on another

Hanne in the *Rainbow Warrior* engine room.

protest boat during the day doing some gas welding. That night I decided to go for a walk – I just had this urge to get off the *Rainbow Warrior* … I can't explain it. I came back at midnight and was stopped by police on the wharf who said there'd been some explosions. I thought, 'Had I forgotten to turn the gas off?'

I didn't even realise the *Warrior* had sunk at first. The crew were all huddled in blankets on the wharf and I still didn't realise what had happened even though they all told me. It wasn't until morning when I saw the boat that it really hit me hard. The first bomb blew a huge hole in the engine room – you could drive a car through – and the crew scrambled ashore as the boat sank.

The next bomb exploded on the propeller shaft, close to my cabin. It was then the crew realised that the ship's photographer, Fernando Pereira, was missing. He had returned to his cabin to get his camera and was drowned.

Rainbow Warrior after the bombing.

These people were my friends, like family ... we'd all been through some intense things and trusted each other with our lives. Now they'd sunk our ship and killed one of our friends. After the bombing, the Greenpeace office was flooded with clothes, sleeping bags, and offers of homes to stay in. You couldn't have had a stronger expression from the people of the world. Our aim back then was to save the world – not thinking that 15 people on a boat could save the world, but that this was our little piece in a big puzzle ...

> 'It matters what every single
> one of us does.'
> Hanne Sorensen

The bombing was the first international terrorist act in New Zealand and the French government had to pay millions of dollars to Greenpeace in compensation. But the spies never faced justice for murdering Fernando.

France eventually stopped testing its weapons – altogether it had exploded nearly 200 nuclear bombs in the Pacific. New Zealanders also protested against the visits of nuclear warships and submarines. In Auckland masses of small boats blocked nuclear vessels from entering the harbour. The government set up a nuclear-free zone around the country which remains today.

The *Rainbow Warrior* was cleaned up and it is now an artificial reef off the New Zealand coast, once again bringing life to the oceans.

> 'There is global insecurity, nations are
> engaged in a mad arms race, spending
> billions of dollars wastefully
> on instruments of destruction,
> when millions are starving.'
> Desmond Tutu

Events

1946–58	American nuclear tests conducted
1952	Britain's first nuclear test in Australia
1954	American nuclear test near Rongelap
1966	France begins nuclear tests on Mururoa
1972	Protest boats sail to Mururoa
1973	World Court rules France has to stop testing
1985	*Rainbow Warrior* bombed by France Fernando Pereira dies during the attack
1987	New Zealand declared nuclear-free
1996	France stops its nuclear tests

Find out more

Read: *Eyes of Fire – The Last Voyage of the Rainbow Warrior* by David Robie, Asia Pacific Network, 2005.

Watch: *When A Warrior Dies* (NZ, 1991).

Online: Nuclear Test Timeline (The Atom Project) www.theatomproject.org/en/about/nuclear-weapons-testing-timeline/

....

Bikini Atoll testing photo credit: US National Archives. *Rainbow Warrior* engine room photo credit: Hanne Sorensen. *Rainbow Warrior* after bombing photo credit: Greenpeace, NZ. Hanne Sorensen quote credit: author interview. Desmond Tutu quote credit: Nobel Lecture at Oslo City Hall, 10 December 1984.

Tank Man

THE STORY OF THE TANK MAN IS ONLY A FEW MINUTES of history, but it best captures the spirit of the peace warrior. University students in China had been protesting peacefully since 1986 demanding more freedom from the government. Then one day in 1989 they marched into Tiananmen Square, Beijing, the largest public square in the world. The students were joined by about half a million people from all walks of life. The army was sent in to clear the square and killed hundreds of innocent people.

The next day army tanks were still patrolling the square like metallic cyclops, and that's when Tank Man made his stand ...

It is 1989 ...

A line of army tanks rumbles down the Avenue of Eternal Peace inside Tiananmen Square. A lone man carrying shopping bags walks briskly across the empty square. He stops and faces the barrel of the leading tank which is rattling towards him. It brakes, bringing all the other tanks to a standstill. The tank turns, trying to drive around the man, but he side-steps and moves with it, blocking the tank's path again.

This mesmerising dance goes on for a short time and then the tank turns off its engine. There is silence in the square. The man leaps on top of the tank and bangs on the hatch. He jumps down and blocks the tank again. The tank's engine fires up and the dance resumes. Eventually people run over and gently lead the man away, out of the square.

Why wasn't Tank Man shot or arrested? He could easily have become another victim of the government crackdown, but his silent protest was being watched. There were international journalists visiting the city and the scene of man versus tank was being filmed. The journalists quickly hid the film in a toilet and it was later smuggled out of China. Images of Tank Man soon appeared on television in billions of homes around the world. Tank Man's face is barely seen in the pictures, his name remains a mystery, and he disappeared after the protest.

Tank Man became a famous peace warrior, inspiring masses of people who were protesting for peace around the world. He was named one of the 100 most influential people of the century by *Time* magazine and yet he's almost unknown within China – the government controls the media and internet, and the Tank Man story and pictures remain blocked to this day.

> 'Peace can only last where
> human rights are respected …'
> 14th Dalai Lama

Events

1949	People's Republic of China created
1986–87	Student demonstrations against the government
1989	Seven weeks of mass protests in Tiananmen Square and in cities around China

Find out more

Watch: *Tank Man*, PBS *Frontline* documentary (US, 2006).

....

Tank Man illustration credit: Hugh Todd.
Dalai Lama quote credit: Nobel Lecture at Oslo City Hall, 11 December 1989.

Opposite: Martin Luther King, Jr. quote credit: *Strength to Love* by Martin Luther King, Jr., Hodder & Stoughton, 1964.

Are we killer apes?

HUMANS HAVE INVENTED SOME MONSTROUS WEAPONS and there's always a war somewhere in the world. So are we naturally violent? After all, evolution tells us that it's the strongest who will survive. In fact humans are just as capable of loving actions as they are of violence (and the same is true of apes). Most humans are reluctant to harm others: for example, many soldiers in the Second World War avoided firing at the enemy.

Violent people are not always the strongest – peace warriors show great strength in facing up to weapons. And being violent is not a recipe for long-term survival. Cooperation is more helpful for successful evolution.

We always have a choice about how we will act. Most of us will probably never have to risk our lives in war or protest, but every day we have to choose whether or not to respect other people:

> Buddha: 'Hate ceases by love; this is an old rule.'
>
> Jesus: 'Love your enemies. Do good to those who hate you.'
>
> Martin Luther King, Jr: 'Hate cannot drive out hate. Only love can do that.'

Blood and Bombers

WHY WOULD A 22-YEAR-OLD PUT HER LIFE IN DANGER just for a peace protest? It started when Moana Cole was a child. She was born in New Zealand but grew up in Australia where her parents fought for the rights of the Aboriginal people. Her mother encouraged the young Moana to write letters to support people who were in prison because of their beliefs ('prisoners of conscience'). Moana saw that her parents always stood up for people in need, and as a teenager she and some friends protested against nuclear warships visiting Brisbane, Australia. They blocked a road with a net they called a 'web of life', which represented the connection between all living things, and Moana was arrested for the first time in her life.

She went to live in Washington in her early twenties and worked with a community group that helped the homeless. The United States army was about to lead a war against Iraq known as the First Gulf War. Moana and three friends decided that they had to protest because they knew that many innocent civilians would be killed by the war. Their idea was to draw attention to the nuclear-armed bombers at Griffiss Air Force Base in New York State.

The huge B-52 warplanes were designed to drop multiple bombs and burning napalm, and to fire missiles with names such as 'The Peacekeeper'. Moana's group wanted their protest to expose these weapons as killing machines. They wanted to show that the primary purpose of a weapon is to spill blood, not to bring peace. So they decided that blood would be their symbol, and each drew some of their own blood to take with them to Griffiss.

They knew that entering an army base without permission was extremely risky. They'd have to walk across a 'deadly force' area where soldiers were allowed

B-52 bomber at Griffiss Air Force Base, US, 1991.

to shoot intruders. They would certainly be arrested and could possibly be killed, but they were prepared to take the consequences. The day of the protest arrived …

It is 1991 …

The four friends arrive at the air force base at six in the morning and split into pairs. They enter the base at opposite ends of the runway. Moana and her friend, Ciaron O'Reilly, can see the bombers in the distance, like sleeping birds of prey. There's no going back now as they step onto the runway – they're already in trouble. Moana had been scared before the protest but somehow it feels right to be here.

She and Ciaron take out their bottles of blood and kneel. They pour the blood on the runway in the shape of a cross. Then they spray-paint the words, 'No more bombing of children. Love your enemies.' They take out small hammers and begin to chip the edge of the runway. Security vehicles drive past, but strangely they don't notice the two protesters for an hour. Finally an air force worker approaches them.

'Keep your hands visible and don't move,' he says.

A military police car races towards them, and before the car has stopped, men with guns leap out and sprint across the runway.

'On the ground!' one yells. 'Face down! Now!'

Moana and Ciaron quickly lie down on the cold tarmac. Within seconds the men reach them. Towering above Moana are several soldiers not much older than she is.

Peace Warriors

> *These guys are hyped, she thinks, like they're in an action movie – they are going to shoot us. Tiny stones dig into her cheek. But instead of fear, she feels at peace.*
>
> *Moana hears a thump and a cry of pain from Ciaron alongside her.*
>
> *'Say a word and I'll blow your f–ing head off,' a soldier barks at him. 'Where are your bombs?' he asks.*
>
> *Ciaron thinks it's best to reply even though he's also been told not to say a word. 'You've got the bombs,' he says, 'that's why we're here.'*
>
> *'Shut up!' yells the soldier.*

The soldiers took Moana and Ciaron away to join their two friends who'd already been caught hammering on the underbelly of a B-52 bomber. All four appeared in court a few days later charged with 'destruction of property' and 'sabotage' – the maximum prison sentence being 15 years. They were held in prison for four months until the trial began.

The young protesters defended themselves in court, arguing that they were trying to draw attention to the victims of the Gulf War. Ramsey Clarke (who'd been a US Attorney General) spoke to support them in court, saying that thousands of innocent civilians had already been killed in the war.

The army's lawyer asked Moana why she'd hammered on the runway, saying that it was 'a violent act' for someone who was supposed to be peace-loving. Moana replied that weapons of war were the real objects of violence, and that her action was symbolic and not intended to harm people. The four friends were found guilty and sentenced to twelve months in prison plus an $1,800 fine. They served their whole time in a crowded county jail.

Today Moana Cole is a lawyer in Christchurch, New Zealand, and she sometimes defends peace protesters in court. She doesn't regret her action in America, saying, 'It's one of the most important things I've done with my life.'

Events

1990–91	First Gulf War: 20,000–35,000 killed
1991	Protest at Griffiss Air Force Base
2003–10	Second Gulf War: about 100,000 killed
2001–12	Afghanistan War: about 60,000 killed
2014	Bombing of Iraq begins again

Find out more

Online: Peace and Disarmament Education Trust
www.lestweforget.org.nz

Online: Timeline of War in the Gulf
www.news.bbc.co.uk/2/hi/middle_east/861164.stm

B-52 bomber photo credit: US National Archive.
Moana Cole quote credit: author interview.

Can you be peaceful and angry?

ANGER IS A NORMAL FEELING. LIKE ALL OUR EMOTIONS, it's not good or bad. What matters is how we act when we feel angry.

The great peace musician Pete Seeger said that anger and love are like the two sides of the same coin. You feel angry when you see people suffering injustice – and that's often what drives you to take action and help them. But anger can also lead to aggressive and violent action. Protest is wrong when people are harmed. It takes self-control to protest peacefully in the face of force.

The people in this book show that peacemaking is not weak, nor is it an excuse to do nothing. Peacemaking requires action and determination. Peace warriors don't withdraw from conflict, but they are often in the thick of it, offering non-violent solutions.

Find out more

Song: 'Letter to Eve' by Pete Seeger
Online: Nobel Peace Prize winners www.nobelprize.org

Dictators

Hitler's Birthday

THERE WAS ONLY ONE mass public protest march in Nazi Germany during the Second World War, and it was by a group of women.

The Nazis and their leader, Adolf Hitler, had been terrorising the Jewish people throughout the 1930s. Hitler thought the Jews were sub-human and said they were to blame for Germany's problems. He

Adolf Hitler, 1943.

ordered the mass murder of Jews everywhere. Before the war began Hitler wrote, 'Nature is cruel; therefore we are also entitled to be cruel.'

Peace Warriors

The only law that saved some Jews from death was being married to a German, but that changed in 1943 when Hitler wanted the city of Berlin finally 'cleansed' of all Jews in time for his birthday. In the weeks beforehand, the Final Roundup of Jews in Berlin began. It applied to Jewish men married to German women.

Hitler's secret police locked up 2,000 Jewish men on a street called Rosenstrasse. The day after the arrests, hundreds of women gathered on street. They had no leaders and no weapons, but they did have a fierce determination to get their men back …

It is 1943 …

The small group of unarmed women march along Rosenstrasse and stop outside the prison building. A line of police armed with machine guns stands guard in front of the main doors. The wives begin a chant, 'We want our husbands back!' It is an incredibly brave act because it breaks two Nazi laws: public demonstrations are banned, and anyone trying to help Jews can be executed.

The police step forward, raise their guns, and fire warning shots into the air. The women are scared and reluctantly return to their homes.

The next day they return in greater numbers and again confront the police line. The following day the crowd of protesters grows larger, until by the end of the week there are thousands of women gathered on Rosenstrasse.

Each day they sing and chant for the release of their Jewish men. The women persist until finally the guards aim their machine guns directly at them.

'If you don't go now, we'll shoot,' an officer yells at the crowd.

The women yell back, 'Murderers! Murderers!'

It's a stand-off. Neither side is willing to act.

Worried that the protest would spread, the Nazi leaders ordered that the Jewish men be released and become free men once again. It was one of the only times when the ruthless leadership backed down. The Holocaust archive, Yad Vashem, has recorded similar stories of 19,000 non-Jews who risked their lives to help Jews escape death during the war.

> 'He who saves one life, it is as if he saved an entire world.'
>
> Jewish Talmud

Events

1933	Nazi Party rule begins in Germany
1939–45	Second World War, and 6 million Jews murdered in the Holocaust
1943	Rosenstrasse protest marches
1946	Nuremberg trials of Nazi leaders for war crimes

Find out more

Read: *The Righteous: The Unsung Heroes of the Holocaust* by Martin Gilbert, Henry Holt & Company, 2003.

Online: Holocaust Centre of New Zealand
www.holocaustcentre.org.nz

Online: Yad Vashem: The Righteous Among the Nations
www.yadvashem.org

....

Adolf Hitler photo credit: Bundesarchiv, Bild 101I-811-1881-31/Wagner/CC-BY-SA) German Federal Archives. Hitler quote credit: *The Voice of Destruction* by Hermann Rauschning, G P Putnam's Sons, 1940.

Facing the Generals

IMAGINE YOU HAVE NO SAY OVER WHO RUNS YOUR country, and when you protest you're beaten up and put in prison. This happened in Burma where army generals ran the country for 50 years. They kept people living in poverty, forced children to work, and locked away anyone who dared to stand up to them. But many brave people did just that.

For many years it was university students who protested against the military rulers. Then in 1988 the students were joined by people from all walks of life in the biggest protest march ever in Burma. About one million ordinary Burmese marched peacefully through the streets of Rangoon city over five days. The protesters wore red bandanas as a symbol of non-violent resistance. But the army moved in and fired at the crowd, killing thousands of unarmed people. Doctors and nurses from the hospital rushed out to help the wounded and they too were shot at. Many of the young student protesters were put in prison for 20 years.

A woman named Aung San Suu Kyi became the greatest sign of hope in Burma. She helped to start a democracy party (NLD) in 1989 with the aim that people could one day choose their own government, but this was a threat to the ruling generals because she dared to speak against them in public. She was put under house arrest (imprisoned in her own home), which lasted for almost 20 years. She was separated from her family who were living in England.

NLD won an election in 1990 but the military rulers simply ignored the votes and kept control of the country. Aung San Suu Kyi won a Nobel Peace Prize but was not allowed to leave Burma to collect it.

Huge crowds of students protested again in 1996, but they were brutally beaten by the army. Again, in 2006, Buddhist monks led a series of protest marches and many of them were also imprisoned. People and governments around the world protested against the injustice in Burma, and Aung San Suu Kyi was finally released from house arrest.

> 'They can't stop the people;
> they can't stop freedom.'
> Aung San Suu Kyi

FACING THE GENERALS

Flag of the National League For Democracy (NLD Party).

Freedom started to emerge in Burma. The generals released hundreds of protesters who'd been in prison since 1988, peaceful marches were allowed, non-government newspapers were published for the first time, and the democracy party won a place in the government.

Aung San Suu Kyi believes that people have the power to change things themselves. Burma is still one of the poorest countries in the world, but she remains hopeful that things will continue to change.

Events

1962   Army generals take over Burma
1988   Student protests are crushed

1989   Aung San Suu Kyi put under house arrest
2010   First free elections held in Burma
2010   Aung San Suu Kyi released

Find out more

Online: Aung San Suu Kyi profile http://www.bbc.com/news/world-asia-pacific-11685977

Read: *Letters from Burma* by Aung San Suu Kyi, Penguin, 2010.

Watch: 'A Conversation with Aung San Suu Kyi' by John Pilger, interview (1996).

....

Aung San Suu Kyi quote credit: 'A Conversation With Aung San Suu Kyi' by John Pilger, 1996 interview. 'Loving Humans' quote credit: *Hard Times Require Furious Dancing* by Alice Walker, New World Library, 2010.

Albert Camus quote credit on page 84: 'After Hiroshima: Between Hell and Reason', *Combat* magazine, 8 August 1945.

from Loving Humans
For Aung San Suu Kyi

ALICE WALKER

Loving humans
is tricky
sometimes
a slap
in the face
is all you get
for doing it
just right.

Does people power always work?

No. Peaceful gatherings are sometimes crushed by the force of the police or the army. Many unarmed protesters have been wounded and killed by government forces. And perhaps worst of all, if protests turn violent, it can lead to all-out war in a country, as happened in Syria in 2013. People power must remain non-violent if it's to lead to peaceful change.

Avoiding violence is difficult when people are angry. That's why peaceful protesters often set themselves apart from violent mobs by openly displaying signs of peace: by linking arms, singing, sitting down, holding banners or wearing symbolic clothing. One protest group in Turkey is famous for reading books while they protested.

People power is most successful when it's organised. For example, in the Philippines, a political party organised protests and the election of a new president. Change can take a long time, and sometimes peaceful protest is just a step forward along the way.

'Peace is the only battle worth waging.'
Albert Camus

The Yellow Revolution

A POWERFUL DICTATOR RULED THE PHILIPPINES FOR 20 years, so how did its poor and unarmed people stand up to him? President Marcos kept control by fear, stealing public money and using the army to beat down anyone who tried to resist him. Over 2 million Filipinos resisted Marcos in one of history's largest non-violent campaigns.

The people first rose up in protest after President Marcos ordered the murder of a popular political leader, Benigno Aquino, Jr., in 1983. Inspired by the song 'Tie a Yellow Ribbon Round the Ole Oak Tree', Benigno's supporters had tied yellow ribbons along the streets of the capital city, Manila, to welcome him home from overseas. Benigno never saw the ribbons – as he walked down the steps of the plane, he was shot dead by police.

Shocked by the assassination, thousands of people marched in the streets of Manila. The army fired tear

Peace Warriors

gas at them, and killed many protesters. After that Filipinos chose yellow as the colour of their protest marches and office workers would shower the streets with yellow confetti every day. The Yellow Revolution had begun.

President Marcos held an election on 7 February 1986, and his main rival was a woman: Corazon Aquino, the widow of the murdered Benigno. Corazon got more votes, but Marcos ignored the result and declared himself the winner. This shameless cheating made Filipinos even more angry. Over a million people held a rally to support Corazon Aquino.

Two weeks later Marcos' generals turned against him, taking over an army base. When his forces threatened to attack the base, church leader Cardinal Jamie Sin went on the radio and called for Filipinos to gather on the streets to protest. It was a Saturday. By Monday night everything had changed ...

It is 1986 ...

Early on Sunday morning the army destroys the radio station's transmission tower. The station switches to an emergency transmitter. Hundreds of thousands of unarmed people respond to the radio call and crowd into a main street in Manila. People bring their children and there is singing, dancing and good spirits. President Marcos sends troops, planes and tanks to the area but tens of thousands of people march to meet them. The people link arms and block the roads to try and stop the troops from moving forward. Protesters tie yellow ribbons around the guns, nuns kneel down in front of the tanks, and others even hug the soldiers. Officers order the crowds to let the army through, but the people stand their ground. The army retreats.

Students block the road in Manila, 1986.

As the day goes on the crowds on the main street grow to almost 2 million people. Helicopter gunships are sent in, but the pilots decide to join the protesters' side and land amongst cheering crowds. More and more soldiers are changing sides.

On Monday, Marcos leaves the country and escapes to Hawaii. On Tuesday, Corazon Aquino is sworn in as the new President.

Peace Warriors

Events

1965	Rule of President Marcos begins
1983	Benigno Aquino, Jr. assassinated
1986	Marcos wins election by fraud
	Marcos flees to the United States, and Corazon Aquino becomes president

Find out more

Online: Corazon Aquino http://www.coryaquino.ph/
Online: Civic Voices People Power http://civicvoices.org

....
Student protest photo credit: Hugh Todd.

Protest

Salt versus Bullets

IT SOUNDS UNBELIEVABLE BUT ORDINARY TABLE SALT helped change the history of a whole country. It was the idea of the most famous peace warrior in the world, Mohandas Gandhi. He became known as Mahatma Gandhi, meaning 'great soul', and his non-violent battle against British rule in India has inspired peacemakers ever since.

It was the 1920s and the British had been in control of India for over a century – the Indian people were desperate to get their country back. Gandhi spent time in South Africa, where he developed a non-violent way of protest called *Satyagraha*. Back in India, he started leading protests including street marches and refusing to buy British goods and services. But the British army fought back by killing hundreds of unarmed demonstrators. Gandhi was imprisoned for two years.

Peace Warriors

His next move was his most daring. In 1930 Gandhi devised a plan for Indians to disobey unfair laws. He decided to target a law called the Salt Tax which gave the British control of the salt market. Indians were forced to pay the British for salt, they weren't allowed to make or sell their own salt, and people weren't even allowed to collect it for free from the seashore. Gandhi knew this law was wrong because salt was essential for health in the hot Indian climate. If only he could mobilise India's huge population to disobey the law alongside him ...

It is 1930 ...

Mahatma Gandhi and a small group of friends walk along a dusty road out of their village. They intend marching across India to the sea to collect salt, gathering supporters as they go. Gandhi wonders if anyone will bother to join them. People laughed at him when he first suggested using salt to fight the mighty British army: 'Bullets will beat salt,' they said. But Gandhi knows he has something more powerful on his side – the truth.

The group walks on and on, and day after day their numbers build. From every city, town and village, thousands of people pour out to join the march. Tens of thousands line the roadsides to watch the procession pass.

Gandhi is full of hope when he finally sees their destination – the seaside village of Dandi. He's exhausted after walking nearly 400 kilometres but he knows he must press on with the protest while the crowd is still with him. He goes quickly to the shoreline, where newspaper journalists surround him.

Gandhi kneels and scoops up a handful of salty mud, saying, 'Without salt, the people cannot live.' He starts a fire and boils the muddy seawater to make salt, and in that action he breaks the law. He says to the journalists, 'Tomorrow, multitudes of people will break the salt laws – it remains to be seen if the government will allow it.'

Then he turns and asks the crowd to join him in making peaceful war against the unfair Salt Tax. Gandhi hopes that people everywhere in India will copy him and that the news will spread around the world. Most of all he prays that the British will not respond with bullets.

Mahatma Gandhi.

Gandhi's idea of rejecting the Salt Tax quickly spread throughout the whole of India. For the next month millions of people protested by collecting and making illegal salt, and also buying and selling salt. But the police brutally beat the peaceful demonstrators and about 70,000 people were arrested. Gandhi was sleeping under a mango tree outside Dandi when 30 armed police came and arrested him.

Despite the crackdown, the people's protest continued for a whole year. Gandhi's action at Dandi had given Indians hope and it started the push that led to independence. Gandhi was shot and killed only a few months after India finally became free from the British Empire.

'Mankind has to get out of violence only through non-violence.'

Mahatma Gandhi

Events

1750	British begin their invasion of India
1858	British rule begins in India
1906	Mahatma Gandhi leads non-violent protests in South Africa
1930	Salt March in India
1947	India becomes independent from Britain
1948	Mahatma Gandhi assassinated

Find out more

Online: India, Defying the Crown
www.aforcemorepowerful.org/films/afmp/stories/india.php

Read: *Gandhi, The Young Protester Who Founded a Nation* by Philip Wilkinson, National Geographic Society, 2007.

....
Mahatma Gandhi photo credit: Agence Meurisse. Gandhi quote credit: *Harijan* journal, 1946.

Should peace protesters break the law?

Many of the peace protesters in this book disobeyed laws. They marched illegally, refused to join the army, or rejected government laws.

Why did they break laws? Because the laws were unfair. They used Gandhi's idea of targeting unjust laws to force change. Governments cannot rule if people do not cooperate by obeying their laws. If millions of people protest like this then a government can be forced to change a law.

All the protesters in this book were prepared to take the consequences of breaking the law – such as paying fines or going to prison. And although they broke laws, they did not harm people during their protests.

'An unjust law is not law at all.'
St Augustine (413 AD)

Little Rock Nine

SOMETIMES PEOPLE ARE MISTREATED SIMPLY BECAUSE their skin is a different colour. Martin Luther King, Jr. had a dream that black and white Americans would one day live together in peace. Slavery had long been abolished but by the 1950s African Americans still did not have the same rights as other citizens – they were treated as lesser humans because of the colour of their skin. The fight to be equal was called the Civil Rights movement. King was the leader of the first large non-violent protest in America. The protest targeted the unjust bus laws in the town of Montgomery in 1955.

The bus laws said black people had to sit at the back of the bus and give up their seats to any white people who wanted to sit down. The protest was sparked by an African American woman, Rosa Parks, who refused to give up her seat and was arrested. She didn't know it but her action would change America forever. Inspired by Rosa, hundreds of black people in the town refused to use the segregated buses for over a year. Shortly after that the Supreme Court abolished the racist bus laws.

Another turning point in the struggle for equal rights was the action of nine high school students, known as the Little Rock Nine. Many schools were segregated until 1957 when the Supreme Court ruled that African Americans could go to any school.

Nine black students enrolled in the all-white Central High School in the town of Little Rock. However, many people in the state were strongly against mixing the races and the governor said 'blood will run in the streets' if the students tried to enter the school. He sent armed guards to the school to stop the Little Rock Nine. The students arranged to meet outside the school but one student, Elizabeth Eckford, arrived at school before the others …

It is 1957 …

Fifteen-year-old Elizabeth Ann Eckford is the first of the nine to arrive at Central High. She is alone, as her mother is at work. Elizabeth walks towards the steps that lead up to the main door of the school. A group of white parents and students spot her and march towards her. They surround Elizabeth and begin chanting,

'Two, four, six, eight … We ain't gonna integrate!'

They wave American flags and signs that read, 'Stop the race mixing!'

Elizabeth keeps on walking, through the crowd and

up the steps to the front door. But she walks into a wall of armed guards who turn her away. She goes back down to the street and towards the shouting protesters.

'Hang the b—!'

Elizabeth looks frantically at the faces in the mob hoping to find someone friendly. She approaches an old woman who might help, but the woman spits on Elizabeth. Feeling trapped, she sits down on a bench. Another woman sits beside her and says kindly, 'Don't let them see you cry.' She guides Elizabeth through the crowd and onto a bus to safety.

The other eight students arrive at school soon after and are also turned back by the guards. The students stay home for two weeks, and then attempt to enter the school again as a group. Another angry crowd meets them and this time a riot breaks out. Three black journalists are attacked and the mob calls for one of the Nine to be hanged. The police hustle the students into cars and speed them away.

The Little Rock Nine were TV news all over America and President Dwight Eisenhower sent in air force troops that night to help them. The next day armed soldiers with jeeps and helicopters escorted the nine students into the school. Some of the troops stayed at school for a year to walk the students between classes. But the soldiers couldn't be everywhere and the Nine were bullied and abused by other students in the playground, toilets and cafeteria. The following year, the governor closed all the high schools in Little

Martin Luther King, Jr. speaking in Washington.

Rock for a year to stop black students attending. The battle for integration in schools was to take many more years.

Martin Luther King, Jr. helped organise many protests and he always insisted on non-violent behaviour by protesters. The biggest Civil Rights march in America was the gathering in Washington of a quarter of a million people, both black and white. It was there that King gave the greatest peace speech in history, in which he talked about his dream of equality: that in the future American people would not be judged by the colour of their skin.

King had to pay a price: his house was bombed, he was beaten up, spied on and put in prison. He also spoke out in public against America's war on Vietnam, calling it 'one of history's most cruel and senseless wars'. King called for a huge march against the war and a few weeks later he was shot dead. The Civil Rights protest movement succeeded in changing many racist laws and winning new rights for African Americans.

Events

1865   Slavery abolished in America
1929   Martin Luther King, Jr. born
1955   Montgomery bus boycott
1957   Little Rock school protest
1963   Civil Rights march in Washington
1964   King awarded Nobel Peace Prize
1968   King assassinated aged 39

Find out more

Online: 'I Have a Dream' speech
https://archive.org/details/MLKDream
Online: Little Rock Nine
www.encyclopediaofarkansas.net

....
Martin Luther King, Jr. photo credit: US National Archives.

The Lions Rage

ONE OF THE WORLD'S FIRST DOCUMENTED AND photographed episodes of people power happened in New Zealand. In 1840 the British took control of New Zealand and signed a peace treaty with the native Māori. The Treaty of Waitangi said that Māori could keep their own land, but the promise was broken. Land was taken from Māori by force, and there were many years of war between the British army and Māori.

One man found a way to fight without spears or guns. Te Whiti was a Māori leader who believed that his people should make peace with their enemies rather than kill them. He wanted to stop the British stealing the land but didn't want to use violence – so he helped set up a peace village, Parihaka. Te Whiti taught the villagers about peaceful resistance, and even the new settlers came to hear him speak.

Parihaka on the morning of the invasion, the villagers sitting centre right, 1881.

Parihaka quickly became one of the largest villages in the country, and the villagers began their non-violent protests against the land-grab: blocking roads around the stolen land and pulling up survey pegs. The government arrested hundreds of protesters and gathered a small army to invade peaceful Parihaka ...

It is 1881...

Te Whiti sits on the ground inside the village. Behind him sit 2,000 men, women and children who live in Parihaka. Warlike sounds erupt from the green hills.

Te Whiti sees hundreds and hundreds of armed soldiers marching along the road towards the village. His chest tightens when he sees a wagon groaning with ammunition. Worse still, on top of the hill, the barrel of a cannon is aimed at them. Te Whiti looks at the villagers. He's told them not to fight back if the soldiers attack – can peace be a shield against bullets and cannon fire?

The column of troops reaches the main gate only to find it blocked by 200 children singing loudly. An officer on horseback gallops straight towards the singing children. He pulls his animal up inches from the choir, spraying dust in their faces.

'Advance!' he orders, and the troops march forward, the lines of children parting neatly. They enter the village but another surprise bars the way: groups of young girls playing with long skipping ropes. The officer has had enough. He leaps off his horse and snatches one end of a skipping rope, but the girl holding the other end jerks the rope from his hands. The enraged officer tackles the girl to the ground, scoops her up and dumps her at the roadside. The troops can barely hide their smiles.

As they march further into the village, women and children walk up to the men and offer fresh bread. A few accept the gift. Finally they arrive at the crowd of 2,000 villagers, and a government minister reads them a warning from the Riot Act:

> All persons unlawfully, riotously, and tumultuously assembled together, to the disturbance of the peace, have one hour to disperse or receive a jail sentence of hard labour for life.

Te Whiti steps forward and says, 'Though the lions rage, still I am for peace.'

The soldiers grab him and he's dragged away.

The village of Parihaka was destroyed by the troops and Te Whiti was imprisoned without a trial. Many of the protesters were put in prison for 20 years. However, inspired by Te Whiti's peaceful stand, people protested against the land-grab for the next hundred years. Finally, after some huge land marches in the 1970s, the government began to return stolen land to Māori and pay them compensation money.

Events

1830	Te Whiti born
1840	Treaty of Waitangi signed between the British Crown and Māori
1860–72	Land Wars: 2,700 people killed
1879–81	Parihaka protests
1907	Te Whiti dies

Find out more

Read: *Parihaka – Peace, Protest and Power* by James Frood, Elizabethan Promotions, 1994.

Online: The Parihaka Story www.parihaka.com

....

Parihaka photo credit: Alexander Turnbull Library, Wellington, New Zealand Ref: PA1-q-183-18.

ARGENTINA

The Disappeared

A 'DIRTY WAR' IS NOT FOUGHT WITH BOMBS BUT WITH fear. The military leaders of Argentina waged a seven-year war against their own people. It was called the Dirty War because tens of thousands of innocent people were imprisoned, tortured or killed. The victims of the war became known as 'the disappeared' because they were kidnapped off the streets and their bodies were never found. How can a Dirty War be resisted? It was the mothers of the disappeared who were the first to stand up to the invisible terror in Argentina. Here's what happened when they dared to speak out ...

It is 1977 ...

Thursday afternoon, and a small group of women stand in the Plaza de Mayo, a square in the centre of

Buenos Aires city. They have already visited the nearby presidential palace to ask where their children are being kept hidden, but the military rulers refused to tell them anything. The mothers are determined to track down their sons and daughters – but what can they do now?

Several armed policemen walk towards the group. This is what the mothers feared would happen: they know it is against the law for more than three people to meet in a public place.

'Go home,' says an officer, 'or you will be arrested for unlawful assembly and disturbing the peace.'

In a flash of inspiration the women link arms in pairs and set off around the plaza. Walking two by two they are no longer breaking the law, and the police have to back off. The mothers' group decides they'll return the following Thursday and continue their protest, expecting the police will be there to watch them. The following week there are a few more mothers at the protest. Again they march around the plaza in support of their disappeared children. Demonstrations are against the law, but a few mothers have stitched the names of their lost children onto white head scarves which they wear as a symbolic protest.

The mothers' group continues to meet in the plaza every Thursday. Slowly their numbers grow until there are hundreds of women walking silently in pairs in protest at their lost children.

The military threatened the marchers with police dogs, and they beat and arrested them. Several leaders of the mothers' group were tortured and executed.

Painted white headscarves at Plaza de Mayo.

But week after week, month after month, the women continued to show up every Thursday in the plaza, and government forces continued to kidnap people.

The Thursday march drew the attention of the world. Thanks to the mothers, everyone now knew about the Dirty War in Argentina, and this put the military dictators under international pressure. The mothers became a symbol of truth in a country where fear ruled. The violent dictatorship fell in 1983 but the mothers' group kept fighting to find out where

Peace Warriors

the bodies of their children were, and to bring those responsible to justice. Only recently have some of the military leaders been tried for their crimes.

The women still march around the Plaza de Mayo every Thursday of every week, as they have done for the past 35 years.

Events

1976	Military dictators take control of Argentina
1977	Mothers' group begins marching
1982	Falklands War between Argentina and Britain
1983	Military dictatorship replaced by a democracy
2010	Military leaders of Dirty War given life imprisonment

Find out more

Online: The Albert Einstein Institution
www.aeinstein.org

....
Plaza de Mayo photo credit: Penelope Todd.

TINA or TARA?

One argument for war is often that 'there is no alternative' (TINA) to military action, but research shows that 'there are realistic alternatives' (TARA) that are more effective. When masses of people join in non-violent action it can bring positive change. Here are a few examples not covered in this book:

1980–89   Poland: Workers protest to demand free trade unions. The Solidarity movement leads to a democratic government.

1988–91   Estonia: The Singing Revolution, in which large gatherings sing banned songs, brings independence from Russia without war.

1983–89   Chile: Creative protests by 700,000 people help to remove a military dictator. They include driving slowly, singing and TV advertisements.

1989   Czechoslovakia: Demonstrations involving 500,000 people led by students and actors bring an end to Communist rule.

1985–94   South Africa: Non-violent protests and resistance were important in undermining the racist Apartheid system.

1998–2000   Serbia: A student group called Otpor! led a non-violent movement that eventually replaced a dictator with a democracy.

THE % SUCCESS AND FAILURE RATES OF 323 LARGE NON-VIOLENT AND VIOLENT RESISTANCE CAMPAIGNS BETWEEN 1900 AND 2006

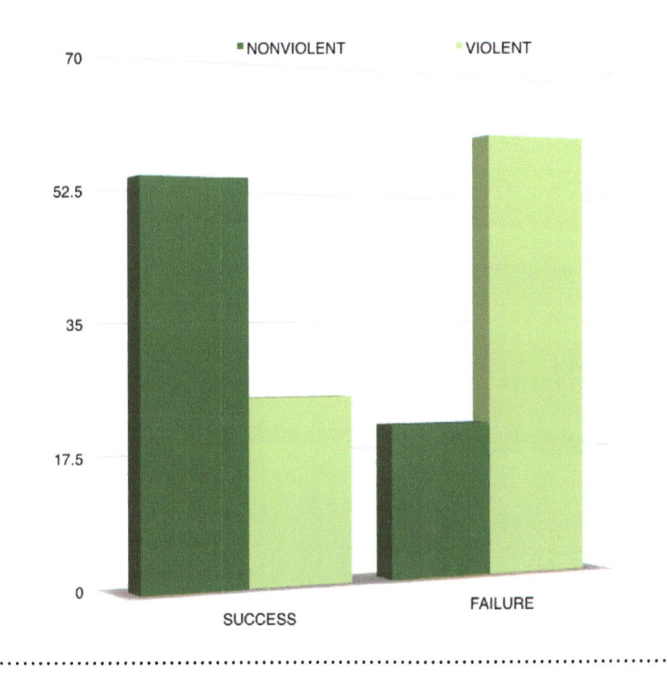

'Between 1900 and 2006, campaigns of non-violent resistance were more than twice as effective as their violent counterparts.'
Erica Chenoweth & Maria J Stephan

....
Quote and graph credit: *Why Civil Resistance Works: The Strategic Logic of Nonviolent Conflict* by Erica Chenoweth and Maria J Stephan. Columbia University Press, 2011.

NEW ZEALAND

To Create not Destroy

Here are the stories of three new zealanders who found creative ways to protest against war.

Lois White

Women in wartime were expected either to look after children or to do jobs that supported the fighting men. These included jobs that kept the war machine going, such as making weapons. Women in New Zealand could not become soldiers until 1970.

Anna Lois White (1902–1984) painted anti-war pictures when most New Zealanders were supporting the war. In the 1920s many young women got married or went teaching but Lois, as she was known, didn't want to follow the crowd. Instead she went to art school and became a well-known painter during the 1930s. At the time many people were without jobs and

Peace Warriors

Civilised by Lois White, 1942.

struggled to feed their families. Lois started including social messages in her art. One painting called *Success* shows a man clutching a bag of money, standing over a starving family.

Her painting *War Makers* was exhibited in 1937 when Europe was piling up weapons for another world war. Lois had painted puppet-like figures: a wealthy politician and two moneymakers dancing around a young soldier and his girlfriend. Lois said the painting was about 'the injustice done to youth' by the older generation who send their children to be killed and wounded in wars.

The painting got a negative reaction because most people thought war was necessary. When the Second World War erupted, Lois produced more paintings with an anti-war message. One is of a town being bombed, civilians forced from their homes and children dying. Lois titled the painting *Civilised* as if to ask, 'Would civilised humans do this to the innocent?'

At the time it was not acceptable for war paintings to show civilians suffering, or dead bodies – the official war art was about soldiers being heroes. Lois was criticised for showing war in its true colours: greed, violence and loss.

Rita Angus

Rita Angus (1908–1970) was another of New Zealand's leading artists. In the 1930s she became a pacifist, knowing this would get her into trouble, because being anti-war was unpopular then. When the Second World War started in 1939, the law required most women to work to support soldiers overseas – making uniforms and ammunition, for example. But Rita did not believe it was right for her to contribute to killing people, no matter how far from the battlefield. Instead she got a job with a peace group, the

Peace Warriors

Woodkraft Cooperative, designing wooden toys.

After that she went fruit picking at the Riverside Community near Nelson, which welcomed anyone opposed to the war. There was no escape from the law, though, and Rita was ordered to report for work in a rubber factory that supplied the army. When she refused, she had to go to court. In her defence she said she could not do work that contributed to the war because she was opposed to violence, and that as an artist her work was 'to create life and not to destroy'. The court ordered her to work but she refused.

After the war, Rita painted pictures about her vision for a peaceful future in a multicultural New Zealand.

> 'Be not dumb, obedient slaves in an army of destruction. Be heroes in an army of construction.'
> Helen Keller

Johnny Johnson

Johnny Johnson (1922–2014) grew up by the sea in Sumner, Christchurch, in the 1930s. His parents were Quakers, a religious group known for their anti-war beliefs, and his father was a soldier in the First World War who'd become a pacifist after seeing the waste of so many young lives. Johnny says, 'I wonder if my father could sense another war coming in 1935 – he sent me to the Quaker school in Wanganui.'

Johnny's own anti-war beliefs strengthened at the Quaker school, but he had to return to Christchurch Boys High School which had a strong military tradition. All New Zealand boys over the age of eleven had to do army training, so it wasn't easy for Johnny at that school.

When the Second World War began he was 18 and had to be officially excused from the army. Johnny got work as an apprentice machinist. One day a job came in that was related to making weapons for the war. Johnny refused to do the work because it was supporting the war, and he was, he says, swiftly 'given the boot'. During his next job working on roads, a fellow employee refused to work with him because Johnny was a conscientious objector.

The New Zealand government treated conscientious objectors much more harshly than other countries did. Men here were usually shut away in camps, while overseas they were allowed to do community work. Then Johnny heard about an aid group called the China Convoy and realised he had mechanical and building skills to offer. Near the end of the war, Johnny and eleven other Kiwi pacifists were given permission by the government to go to China. It was the first such group from New Zealand and they all came from families that were committed to peace.

The China Convoy was a travelling medical group run by the Friends' Ambulance Unit (FAU), a Quaker organisation working in 25 countries and staffed by volunteers who believed in non-violence. Their aim was: 'To build up a new world rather than fighting to destroy the old.'

China had been devastated by Japanese attacks during the Second World War – there was a famine and millions of people had lost their homes. Johnny was 22 when he arrived in China with the FAU. They were all shocked by streets full of starving refugees. There was a cholera epidemic and no medical supplies. Johnny said he often felt helpless in those early days when faced with so many suffering people.

> There was no escaping death and despair. The chilling sight of corpses lying amidst the rubbish outside the city wall ... the terrible sight of people lying about, just absolute skin and bone.

Jonny worked in the transport section of the Convoy, driving supply trucks to small hospitals and clinics in the middle of nowhere, over some of the world's worst roads.

Some big problems had to be faced: the huge size of China, the extremely bad roads, the old trucks and little petrol. Johnny was a driver and a mechanic, a job which was to be dangerous, dirty and lonely – but the Kiwis had a reputation in China for being able to rough it and to fix anything.

He always fixed his own trucks when they broke down in the wilderness, sometimes improvising engine parts using metal scraps found on the roadside. When his truck got stuck in mud or sand, he'd have to find local horses or cows to pull it out.

The rocky Chinese roads were a nightmare for a heavy truck. They were hand-carved from the mountainsides and riddled with holes and gaps. There were many accidents and Johnny often saw smashed vehicles on the valley floors below. Hold-ups were another danger and he once saw soldiers carrying the heads of bandits on poles as a reminder to others of the punishment for theft – beheading.

The Convoy became a lifeline for many people in that time of rebuilding. Johnny said, 'We delivered about 90% of the medicines that came into China.'

In 1947 Johnny returned to Christchurch and he remained strongly anti-war his whole life.

Events

1914	Friends' Ambulance Unit formed in First World War
1940	Conscription re-introduced to NZ in Second World War
1941	Riverside Peace Community formed
1941–46	NZ conscientious objectors held in detention camps

1970   Women allowed to join NZ Defence Forces

Find out more

Read: *By the Waters of Babylon – The Art of A Lois White* by Nicola Green, Auckland City Art Gallery, 1993.

Read: *Rita Angus – An Artist's Life* by Jill Trevelyan, Te Papa Press, 2008.

Read: *Go Anywhere, Do Anything – New Zealanders in the Friends' Ambulance Unit in China 1945–1951*. Editors: Caitriona Cameron & Audrey Brodie. Beechtree Press, 1996.

....

Helen Keller quote credit: 'Strike Against War'. Speech at Carnegie Hall, New York City, 5 January 1916. *Civilised* by Lois White credit: Auckland Art Gallery Toi o Tāmaki, purchased 1992. Accession No. 1992/4/1. Johnny Johnson quote credit: author interview.

Talking about Peacebuilding

More discussion questions

1. PEACE WARRIORS

   Who are the peace warriors in the world today?

   What are some common characteristics that peace warriors share?

   What are some of the big challenges they face?

   Can anyone be a peace warrior?

   Why is peacemaking sometimes seen as weaker than armed response?

   What are the risks in being a peace warrior or peacebuilder?

   What changes would you like to see in the world to make it less violent?

   What steps could you take to help build peace in your community?

2. PEOPLE POWER

Do people-power groups need a leader?

Workers have played key roles in non-violent change – what power do workers have that other people do not?

In what ways do dictatorships and repressive governments rely on people's cooperation?

Why do people-power groups try to get the attention of media?

How can people power be useful in more peaceful countries such as ours?

What organisations work for peace? What are the benefits of working through organised groups? Discuss both government and non-governmental groups.

Is it ever acceptable for protesters to break the law?

What place (if any) does anger have in protesting?

Why are students often at the forefront of non-violent resistance? (For example, in China, Burma, El Salvador, Serbia, Nazi Germany.)

3. War and Weapons

Do you agree that some wars might be 'just'?

Can wars be prevented?

Are humans naturally violent?

What role can the military have as peacekeepers?

Are there non-violent ways to defeat terrorism?

Why are nuclear weapons a more serious threat than other weapons?

In what ways are war and poverty connected?

Find out more

Peacebuilding Toolkit for Educators
www.buildingpeace.org

Civic Voices For Peace
www.civicvoices.org

Peace and Disarmament Education Trust:
www.lestweforget.org.nz

Watch: *Sedition: the suppression of dissent in World War II New Zealand.* (NZ, 2005)

Glossary

British Empire – area once ruled by the United Kingdom, including up to one fifth of the world's population.

Civilian – member of the public, non-military person.

Civil Rights – the right of a citizen to vote and to freely use public services (education, transport, etc).

Conscientious objector – person who refuses to join the army in wartime, usually because they believe it's wrong to kill another human.

Conscription – government law that forces people to join the army.

Democracy – system of government where the leaders of a country are chosen by the people voting every few years.

Dictatorship – where one person or a small group rules a country by force, and keeps control by fear and corruption.

Genocide – deliberate, organised murder of a racial, national or religious group of people.

Gestapo – secret police in Nazi Germany whose job was to find 'enemies of the people' (such as Jews, minorities, activists and homosexuals).

Glossary

Holocaust – the murder of 6 million Jews in the Second World War.

Nazi – short for the 'National Socialist Party', led by Adolf Hitler in Germany.

Nuclear blast – huge explosion created by splitting (or joining) atoms.

Pacifist – person who believes violence is wrong, therefore war is wrong.

Resistance group – secret organisation of civilians that disrupts an oppressive government, usually during wartime.

Satyagraha – Gandhi's belief in non-violent resistance, meaning 'insistence on truth'.

Segregation – separating different races from each other, especially in public places such as schools and transport.

United Nations Peacekeepers – troops and police who go to war-torn countries to help maintain peace.

Buying this book donates money to peacebuilding

Oxfam New Zealand is a non-profit organisation dedicated to finding lasting solutions to poverty and injustice. Oxfam's work to build peace and prevent conflict is part of a wider programme to promote the right to life and security. The approach includes community-based peacebuilding, emergency relief to people affected by conflict, as well as campaigning and advocacy work at an international level.

Oxfam New Zealand has developed strong expertise in conflict prevention and peacebuilding in the Pacific. Oxfam is a part of the Control Arms campaign, which demands that governments toughen controls on the arms trade and implement the new international Arms Trade Treaty, to stop arms being sold to those likely to misuse them.

The author of *Peace Warriors*, Raymond Huber, is donating half his royalties from sales of the book to Oxfam.

Thank you

Peace Warriors has been made possible with a grant from Quaker Peace & Service Aotearoa; inspiration from Moana Cole, Hanne Sorensen and Johnny Johnson who allowed me to interview them, and Professor Kevin Clements who provided the foreword; the generosity of Alison Disbrowe, Hugh Todd, Jane Mountier, Donna Hendry, Mia Tay, Auckland Art Gallery, Penelope Todd and Professor Richard Jackson; and the wisdom of *Nonviolence: The History of a Dangerous Idea* by Mark Kurlansky.

VISIT THE PEACE WARRIORS WEBSITE
TO FIND OUT MORE

www.peacewarriors.nz

'Non-violence' by Carl Fredrik Reuterswärd.
Photo credit: Oxfam NZ.